The Songs of Rodgers & Hammerstein

16 Songs from 10 Musicals

Interior photos provided courtesy of The Rodgers & Hammerstein Organization

ISBN 978-1-4234-7475-3

WILLIAMSON MUSIC®

A RODGERS AND HAMMERSTEIN COMPANY

www.williamsonmusic.com

EXCLUSIVELY DISTRIBUTED BY

HAL•LEONARD®
CORPORATION

7777 W. BLUEMOUND RD. P.O. BOX 13819 MILWAUKEE, WI 53213

Visit Hal Leonard Online at
www.halleonard.com

£16.95

TABLE OF CONTENTS

PERFORMERS ON THE RECORDINGS

Cory Goodrich . . . . Performance Tracks 1, 5, 7, 11-12, 14, 16
Angela Gould . . . . Performance Tracks 3, 4, 6, 9-10, 13, 15
Kathleen Sonnentag . . . . Performance Tracks 2, 8

Richard Walters, pianist for all tracks except accompaniment track 10, played by Reuben Piirainen.

After long and highly distinguished careers with other collaborators, Richard Rodgers (composer) and Oscar Hammerstein II (librettist/lyricist) joined forces to create the most consistently fruitful and successful partnership in the American musical theatre.

Prior to his work with Hammerstein, Richard Rodgers (1902-1979) collaborated with lyricist Lorenz Hart on a series of musical comedies that epitomized the wit and sophistication of Broadway in its heyday. Prolific on Broadway, in London and in Hollywood from the '20s into the early '40s, Rodgers & Hart wrote more than 40 shows and film scores. Among their greatest were ON YOUR TOES, BABES IN ARMS, THE BOYS FROM SYRACUSE, I MARRIED AN ANGEL and PAL JOEY.

Throughout the same era Oscar Hammerstein II (1895-1960) brought new life to a moribund art form: the operetta. His collaborations with such preeminent composers as Rudolf Friml, Sigmund Romberg and Vincent Youmans resulted in such operetta classics as THE DESERT SONG, ROSE-MARIE, and THE NEW MOON. With Jerome Kern he wrote SHOW BOAT, the 1927 operetta that changed the course of modern musical theatre. His last musical before embarking on an exclusive partnership with Richard Rodgers was CARMEN JONES, the highly-acclaimed 1943 all-black revision of Georges Bizet's tragic opera CARMEN.

OKLAHOMA!, the first Rodgers & Hammerstein musical, was also the first of a new genre, the musical play, representing a unique fusion of Rodgers' musical comedy and Hammerstein's operetta. A milestone in the development of the American musical, it also marked the beginning of the most successful partnership in Broadway musical history, and was followed by CAROUSEL, ALLEGRO, SOUTH PACIFIC, THE KING AND I, ME AND JULIET, PIPE DREAM, FLOWER DRUM SONG and THE SOUND OF MUSIC. Rodgers & Hammerstein wrote one musical specifically for the big screen, STATE FAIR, and one for television, CINDERELLA. Collectively, the Rodgers & Hammerstein musicals earned 35 Tony Awards, 15 Academy Awards, two Pulitzer Prizes, two Grammy Awards and 2 Emmy Awards. In 1998 Rodgers & Hammerstein were cited by Time Magazine and CBS News as among the 20 most influential artists of the 20th century and in 1999 they were jointly commemorated on a U.S. postage stamp.

Despite Hammerstein's death in 1960, Rodgers continued to write for the Broadway stage. His first solo entry, NO STRINGS, earned him two Tony Awards for music and lyrics, and was followed by DO I HEAR A WALTZ?, TWO BY TWO, REX and I REMEMBER MAMA. Richard Rodgers died on December 30, 1979, less than eight months after his last musical opened on Broadway. In March of 1990, Broadway's 46th Street Theatre was renamed The Richard Rodgers Theatre in his honor.

At the turn of the 21st century, the Rodgers and Hammerstein legacy continues to flourish, as marked by the enthusiasm that greeted their Centennials, in 1995 and 2002 respectively.

In 1995, Hammerstein's centennial was celebrated worldwide with commemorative recordings, books, concerts and an award-winning PBS special, "Some Enchanted Evening." The ultimate tribute came the following season, when he had three musicals playing on Broadway simultaneously: SHOW BOAT (1995 Tony Award winner, Best Musical Revival); THE KING AND I (1996 Tony Award winner, Best Musical Revival); and STATE FAIR (1996 Tony Award nominee for Best Score.)

In 2002, the Richard Rodgers Centennial was celebrated around the world, with tributes from Tokyo to London, from the Hollywood Bowl to the White House, featuring six new television specials, museum retrospectives, a dozen new ballets, half a dozen books, new recordings and countless concert and stage productions (including three simultaneous revivals on Broadway, matching Hammerstein's feat of six years earlier), giving testament to the enduring popularity of Richard Rodgers and the sound of his music.

THE SONGS & SHOWS

Songs are in Original Keys except where noted.

ALLEGRO
Broadway Opening: October 10, 1947

This original book by Oscar Hammerstein follows the life of Joseph Taylor from his birth in 1905 until 1940. The story focuses on negative consequences of personal greed versus a life of community service.

In Chicago Dr. Joseph Taylor's nurse Emily sings **"The Gentleman Is a Dope"** trying to casually dispel her feelings for him. Though they only have a professional relationship, there is an undeniable connection between them. Soon after Joseph discovers that his materialistic wife is cheating on him; the marriage splits up. He and Emily recognize their romance and decide on a simpler life in a small town where they can care for those who truly are in need.

CAROUSEL
Broadway Opening: April 19, 1945
London Opening: June 7, 1950
Broadway Revivals: 1949, 1954, 1957, 1994
London Revival: 2008
Film Release: February 16, 1956

Based on the play *Liliom* by Ferenc Molnar, *Carousel* is set in a small town on the New England coast, 1873-1888.

Billy Bigelow, Julie's volatile husband, gets mixed up with some thugs and attempts a robbery. Billy is caught by the would-be victim, who vows to hand him over to the police with the prospect of a prison term. Cornered, disgraced and terrified for Julie and their unborn child, Billy stabs himself. He dies in Julie's arms. Nettie Fowler, the maternal figure in the show, sings **"You'll Never Walk Alone"** to give Julie comfort and hope. The song is repeated at the end of the show, years later, at the graduation of Julie and Billy's daughter. The role of Nettie is sung by a classically defined mezzo-soprano. The original key appears in the soprano volume of this series. The practical transposition down for this volume should be useful.

CINDERELLA (television)
First Broadcast (live): March 31, 1957
First Remake for Television, First Broadcast: February 22, 1965
Second Remake for Television, First Broadcast: November 2, 1997

Though never officially on Broadway or in London's West End, stage versions of the musical have been produced since 1961.

Based on the fairy tale, *Cinderella* (source: *Cendrillon, ou la Petite Pantoufle de Vair* by Charles Perrault) was the first original musical written for television. Its original live broadcast in 1957, starring Julie Andrews, drew the largest television audience to date of 107,000,000 people. A new color television version was made in 1965, starring Lesley Ann Warren. The 1997 television film starred Brandy Norwood, with other songs by Rodgers interpolated into the score.

Abused and unappreciated by her stepmother and stepsisters, Cinderella sits by the fireplace alone and sings **"In My Own Little Corner."**

The fairy godmother has magically appeared and enabled Cinderalla to attend the royal ball. The Prince is captivated by her. In love at first sight, Cinderella and the Prince sing **"Ten Minutes Ago"** following their first dance.

Cinderella's stepsisters do not recognize her after her fairytale makeover. They jealously sing **"Stepsisters' Lament"** as they eye the Prince's attention to the mysterious belle of the ball.

Cinderella's songs, originally written for Julie Andrews, have been subsequently transposed for other productions. The keys in this edition should be a comfortable fit for most belters.

FLOWER DRUM SONG

Broadway Opening: December 1, 1958
London Opening: March 24, 1960
Broadway Revival: 2002
Film Release: November 9, 1961

Based on the novel by C.Y. Lee, *Flower Drum Song* takes place in Chinatown of San Francisco. It highlights the generational differences between the young Chinese-Americans and their more traditional parents.

Linda Low, a singer at a local bar, sings **"I Enjoy Being a Girl"** about the attention that she gets from men. She is the girlfriend of Wang Ta and has also captured the heart of Sammy Fong. Both men, pledged to marry the mail-order bride Mei Li, forgo family traditions to woo Linda.

Helen Chao, a seamstress, is in love with Wang Ta, who is engaged to another woman. She sings of her predicament in **"Love, Look Away."** Originally for soprano, this song was transposed down for belter for the 2002 Broadway revival.

THE KING AND I

Broadway Opening: March 29, 1951
London Opening: October 8, 1953
Broadway Revivals: 1977, 1985, 1996
London Revivals: 1979, 2000
Film Release: June 26, 1956
Animated Film Release: March 19, 1999

Based on the novel *Anna and the King of Siam* by Margaret Langdon, the story takes place in Bangkok, Siam, early 1860s. Anna Leonowens is a young widowed teacher from England brought by the king to educate his many children.

Anna finds the King to be intolerably disagreeable. Lady Thiang, the King's chief wife (of many), knows him best. She affectionately relates all his flaws and redeeming qualities to Anna in **"Something Wonderful."** The role of Lady Thiang is sung by a classically defined mezzo-soprano. For this edition, the song has been transposed down a whole step from the original key, making it comfortable for most singers.

ME AND JULIET

Broadway Opening: May 28, 1953

With an original book by Oscar Hammerstein II, *Me and Juliet* is a backstage musical comedy that takes place in and around the theatre where the musical "Me and Juliet," in a pre-Broadway tryout run is playing. Scenes and songs between the characters in the company are interspersed with scenes and songs from the show within the show.

As part of the production of "Me and Juliet" (the musical within the musical), the principal dancers playing the roles Don Juan and Carmen have a number together. Carmen sings the wise-cracking **"We Deserve Each Other"** to Don Juan before an extended dance.

OKLAHOMA!

Broadway Opening: March 31, 1943
London Opening: April 29, 1947
Broadway Revivals: 1951, 1953, 1979, 2002
London Revivals: 1980, 1998
Film Release: October 11, 1955

Oklahoma!, based on the play *Green Grow the Lilacs* by Lynn Riggs, is set in the summer of 1907 just prior to the admission of the Indian territory Oklahoma as a state.

Ado Annie Carnes is an unsophisticated, high-spirited ranch girl whose pa has told Will Parker that if he comes up with $50 he can marry her. Will wins $50 in a rodeo in Kansas City but while he's away Ado Annie agrees to go to the box social with peddler Ali Hakim. Attracted to both men, she sings of her predicament in **"I Cain't Say No."**

THE SOUND OF MUSIC

Broadway Opening: November 16, 1959
London Opening: May 18, 1961
Broadway Revival: 1998
London Revivals: 1981, 2006
Film Release: March, 2, 1965

Set in Austria in 1938 before and during the Anschluss (The Nazi annexing of Austria to Germany), *The Sound of Music* is based on the book *The Trapp Family Singers* by Maria Augusta Trapp. Maria, a young woman intending to become a nun, joins the household of widower Captain von Trapp as governess to his seven children. Maria brings music back into the house. She and the Captain unexpectedly fall in love, ending the Captain's engagement to the Baroness. After Maria and the Captain marry, they escape Austria and the Nazis.

In the film version, **"My Favorite Things"** is sung by Maria to the von Trapp children to distract them during a particularly frightening thunderstorm. In the original stage version, the song occurs much earlier. The Mother Abbess, while chastising Maria for her inattentiveness, asks Maria about a song she has heard the apologetic novice singing. They sing **"My Favorite Things"** together. The song has been transposed into a comfotable key for belters for this volume.

SOUTH PACIFIC

Broadway Opening: April 7, 1949
London Opening: November 1, 1951
Broadway Revivals: 1955, 2008
London Revivals: 1988, 2001
Film Release: March 19, 1958
Film Remake Release (television): March 26, 2001

On a U. S. Naval base in the south Pacific during World War II a romance develops between middle-aged French planter Emile de Becque and young American nurse Nellie Forbush from Little Rock, Arkansas, who is stationed there. The musical is based on two short stories from *Tales of the South Pacific* by James A. Michener.

Emile has invited Nellie to lunch. A romance is blossoming. In high spirits about being away from home and in an exotic place she sings **"A Cockeyed Optimist."**

Nellie realizes how little she knows about the much older Emile, who she learns is a widower, formerly married to a Polynesian woman. She resolves to end the relationship, but a conversation with him convinces her of her emotions for him. She exuberantly sings **"A Wonderful Guy."**

For a follies revue show put on for the troops, Nellie gets into the spirit, dresses as a male sailor, and sings the raucous number **"Honey Bun"** to Luther Billis who is dressed as a hula-skirted native girl.

"Bali Ha'i" is sung by Bloody Mary, a lively native woman, to Lieutenant Joseph Cable. She tries to arouse his interest in her daughter Liat by seductively telling him about a mysterious island, off limits to naval personnel, where the native women have been evacuated.

STATE FAIR (film)

Film Release: August 20, 1945
Film Remake Release: March 15, 1962
Stage Version, Broadway Opening: March 27, 1996

Based on Phil Strong's novel by the same title, *State Fair* takes place in Iowa, 1946. This is Rodgers and Hammerstein's only original film score. The film was released in 1945, and remade in 1962 with a change in the setting to Texas. A stage adaptation opened on Broadway in 1996.

It is August. Farm girl Margy Frake prepares to attend the Iowa Sate Fair with her family. Feeling unsettled and expectant of something to come, she sings **"It Might as Well Be Spring."**

Richard Rodgers (left) and Oscar Hammerstein II

THE GENTLEMAN IS A DOPE
from *Allegro*

Lyrics by Oscar Hammerstein II
Music by Richard Rodgers

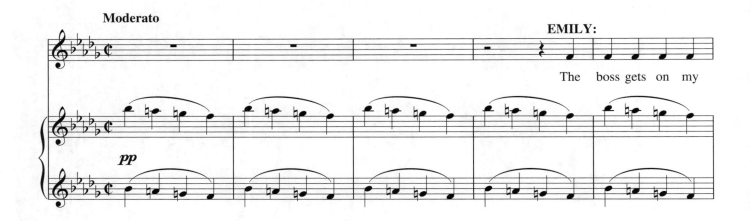

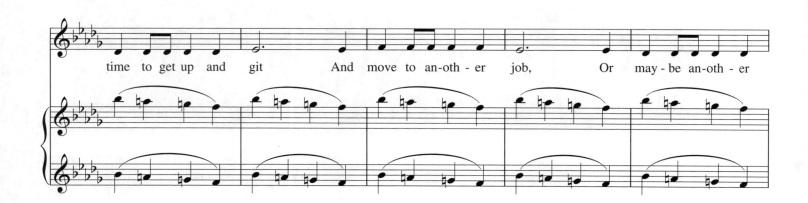

do I get in a dith-er? He does-n't be-long ___ to ___ me! ___

___ The gen-tle-man is-n't bright ___ he does-n't know the score: ___

___ A cake will come, he'll take a crumb and nev-er ask for more. The

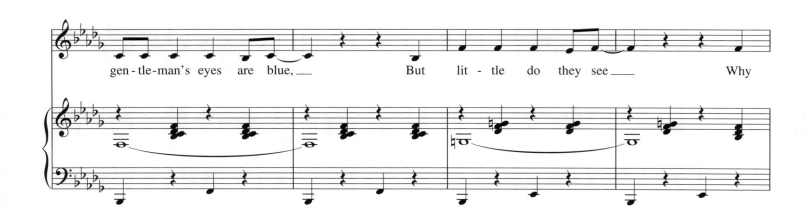

gen-tle-man's eyes are blue, ___ But lit-tle do they see ___ Why

am I beat-ing my brains out? He does - n't be-long ___ to ___ me! _____

___ He's some - bod - y else ___ 's prob - lem, _____ She's

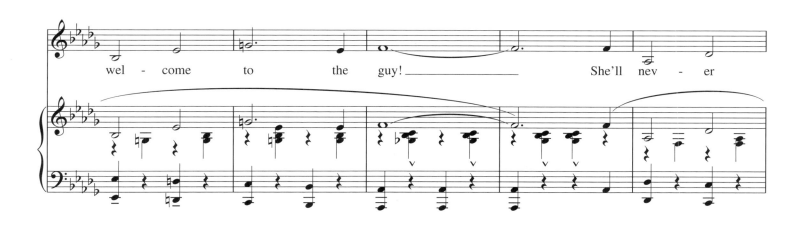

wel - come to the guy! _____ She'll nev - er

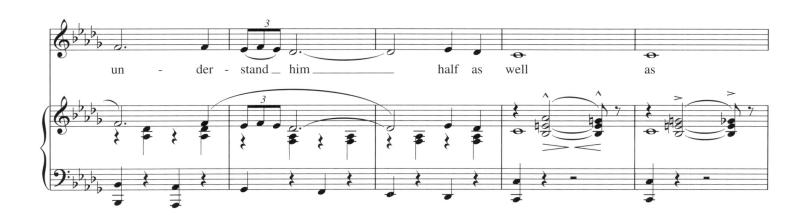

un - der - stand ___ him _____ half as well as

I. _____ The gen-tle-man is a dope __ He

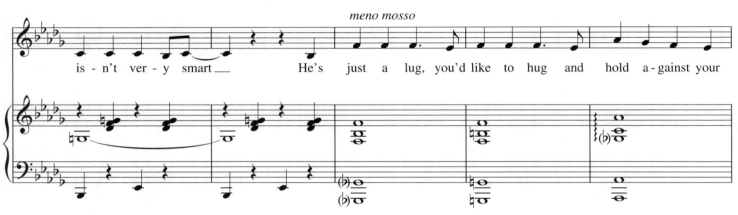

meno mosso

is-n't ver-y smart __ He's just a lug, you'd like to hug and hold a-gainst your

heart. The gen-tle-man does-n't know __ How hap-py he could be __

— Look at me! Cry-ing my eyes out, As if he be-

longed to me! _____ He'll nev - er be - long to

me. (spoken:) Taxi! The gen-tle-man is a dope _

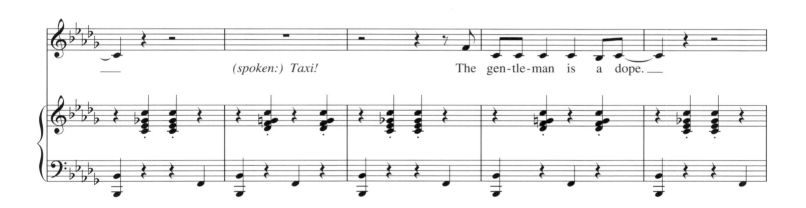

_ (spoken:) Taxi! The gen-tle-man is a dope. _

(spoken:) Oh, hell, I'll walk!

* These spoken lines from the show are optional.

YOU'LL NEVER WALK ALONE

from *Carousel*

Lyrics by Oscar Hammerstein II
Music by Richard Rodgers

IN MY OWN LITTLE CORNER
from *Cinderella*

Lyrics by Oscar Hammerstein II
Music by Richard Rodgers

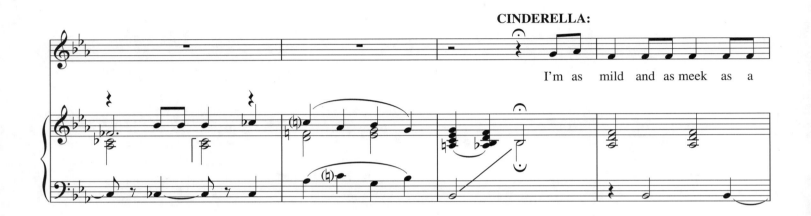

CINDERELLA:

I'm as mild and as meek as a

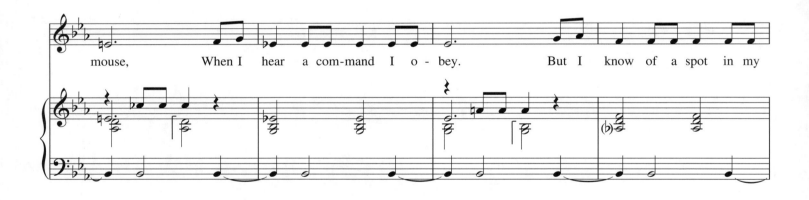

mouse, When I hear a com-mand I o-bey. But I know of a spot in my

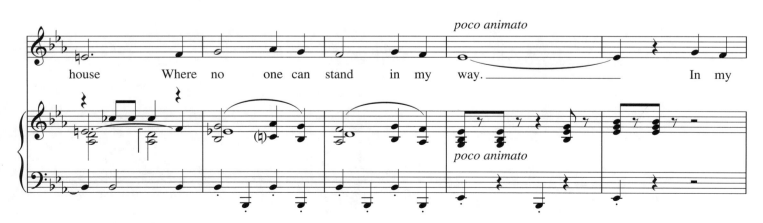

house Where no one can stand in my way. _____ In my

poco animato

own lit - tle cor - ner, in my own lit - tle chair, I can

be what - ev - er I want to be. _____ On the

wing of my fan - cy I can fly an - y - where And the

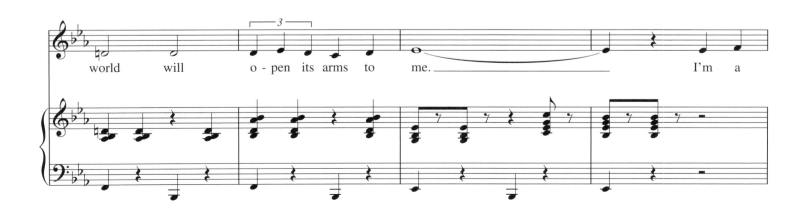

world will o - pen its arms to me. _____ I'm a

young Nor - we - gian prin - cess or a milk maid, _____ I'm the

great - est pri - ma don - na in Mi - lan, _____ I'm an

heir - ess who has al - ways had her silk made _____ By her

own flock of silk - worms in Ja - pan! _____ I'm a

girl men go mad for, Love's a game I can play With a

cool and con - fi - dent kind of air, _____ Just as

long as I stay in my own lit - tle cor - ner, _____ All a -

lone in my own lit - tle chair.

hunt - ress on an Af - ri - can sa - fa - ri _____ (It's a

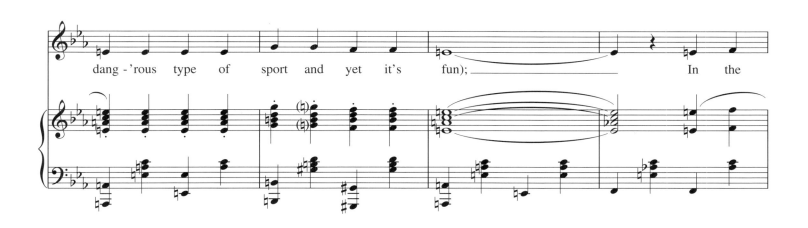

dang - 'rous type of sport and yet it's fun); _____ In the

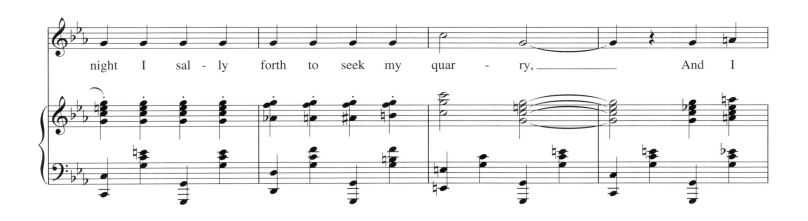

night I sal - ly forth to seek my quar - ry, _____ And I

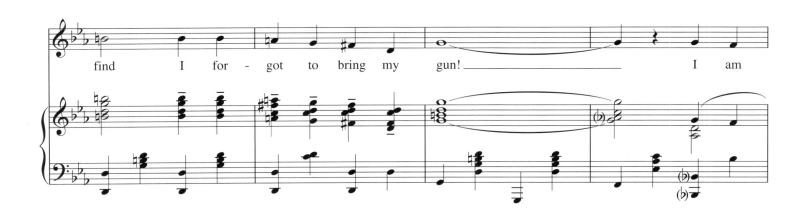

find I for - got to bring my gun! _____ I am

TEN MINUTES AGO

from *Cinderella*

Lyrics by Oscar Hammerstein II
Music by Richard Rodgers

The song is sung twice in the show, first by the Prince, then by Cinderella.

floor. _____ Ten min-utes a-go I met you _____

_ And we mur-mured our how-do-you-do's. _____ I

want-ed to ring out the bells And fling out my arms and to

sing out the news: _____ I have found him! _____ He's an

STEPSISTERS' LAMENT

from *Cinderella*

Lyrics by Oscar Hammerstein II
Music by Richard Rodgers

Why would a fel-low want a girl like her, a frail and fluf-fy beau-ty?

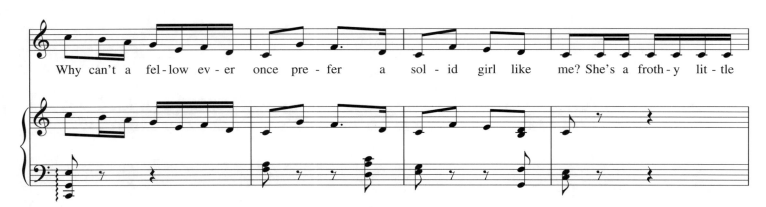

Why can't a fel-low ev-er once pre-fer a sol-id girl like me? She's a froth-y lit-tle

Note: In the show this is sung by both sisters.

cheeks are a pret-ty shade of pink, But not an-y pink-er than a rose is. Her

skin may be del-i-cate and soft, But not an-y soft-er than a doe's is. Her

neck is no whit-er than a swan's. She's on-ly as dain-ty as a dai-sy. She's

on-ly as grace-ful as a bird. So why is the fel-low go-ing cra-zy? Oh,

I ENJOY BEING A GIRL

from *Flower Drum Song*

Lyrics by Oscar Hammerstein II
Music by Richard Rodgers

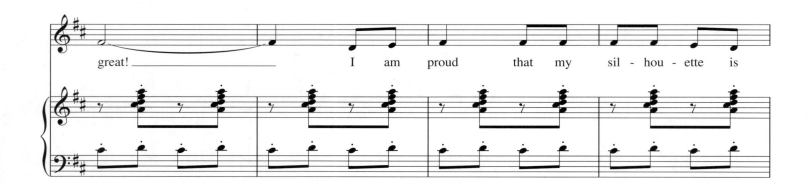

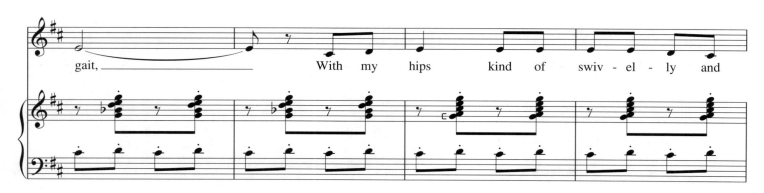

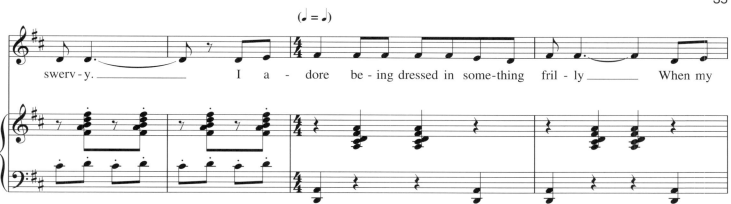

swerv-y. _____ I a - dore be - ing dressed in some-thing fril - ly _____ When my

date comes to get me at my place. Out I go with my Joe or John or Bil - ly, _____ Like a

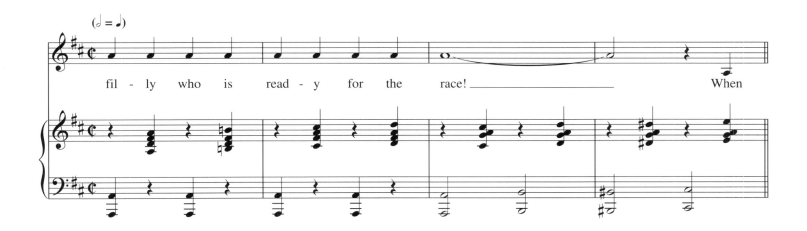

fil - ly who is read - y for the race! _____ When

Brightly

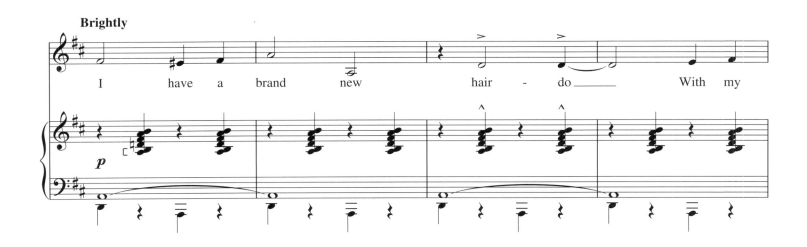

I have a brand new hair - do _____ With my

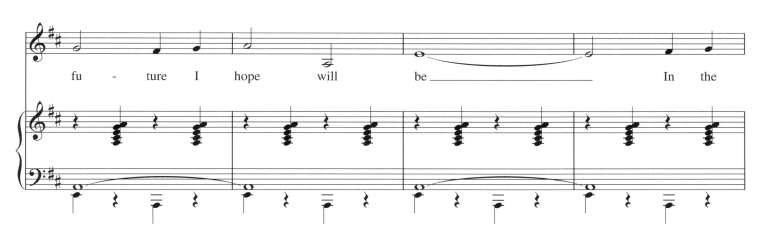

fu - ture I hope will be _____ In the

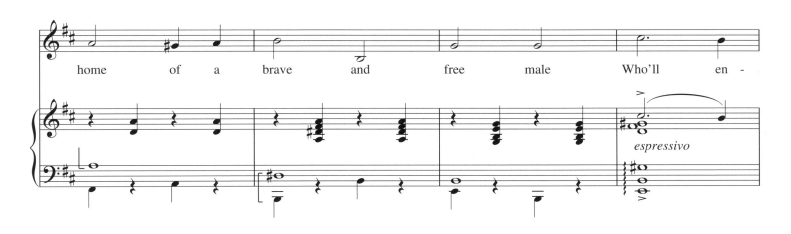

home of a brave and free male Who'll en -

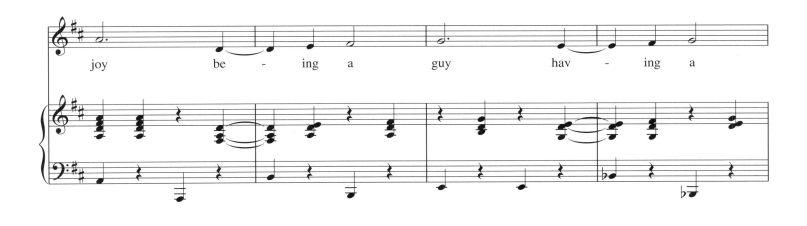

joy be - ing a guy hav - ing a

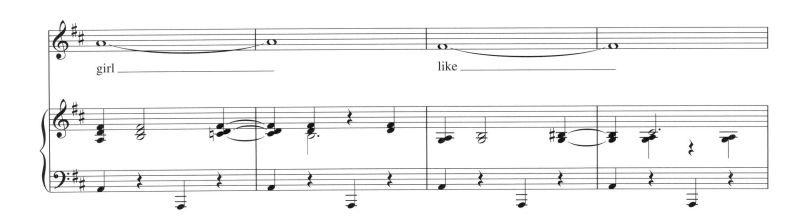

girl _____ like _____

LOVE, LOOK AWAY
from *Flower Drum Song*

Lyrics by Oscar Hammerstein II
Music by Richard Rodgers

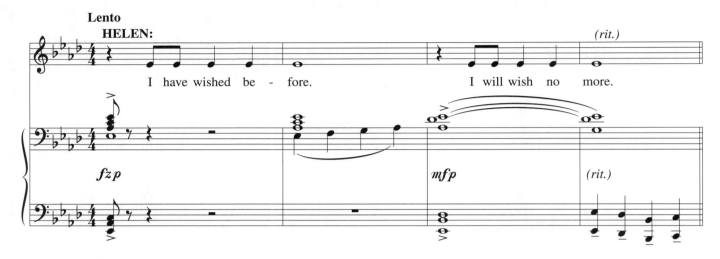

I have wished be - fore. I will wish no more.

Love, look a - way! Love, look a-way from me.

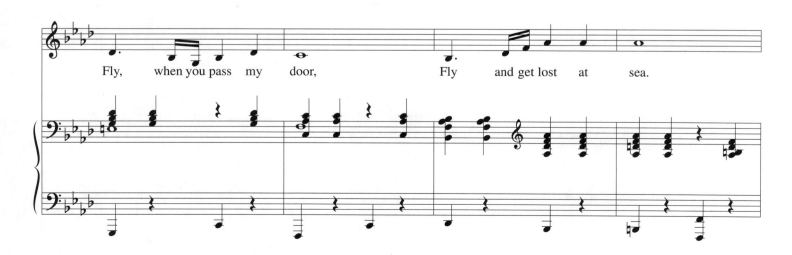

Fly, when you pass my door, Fly and get lost at sea.

Call it a day._____ Love, let us say we're through.

No good are you for me, No good am I for you.

Want-ing you_____ so, I try too much._____

mf

Af - ter you_____ go, I cry too much._____

The optional notes, for the final time, are editorial suggestions.

SOMETHING WONDERFUL
from *The King and I*

Lyrics by Oscar Hammerstein II
Music by Richard Rodgers

48

WE DESERVE EACH OTHER

from *Me and Juliet*

Lyrics by Oscar Hammerstein II
Music by Richard Rodgers

Let me tell you, broth-er, I am a dif - fi-cult girl. ___

You're an im - pos - si-ble char - ac - ter, ___ Why don't we give it a

whirl? I don't want ___ to re - form you, ___ To

make your mis - takes ___ you are free. But I just want ___ to be

I CAIN'T SAY NO

from *Oklahoma!*

Lyrics by Oscar Hammerstein II
Music by Richard Rodgers

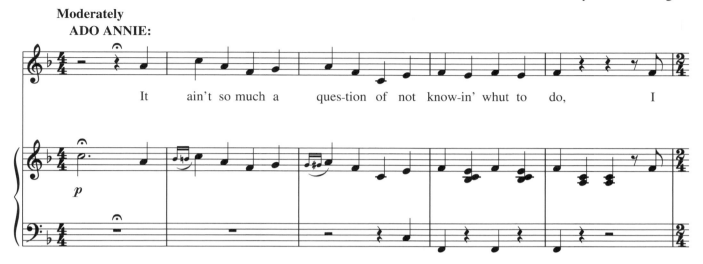

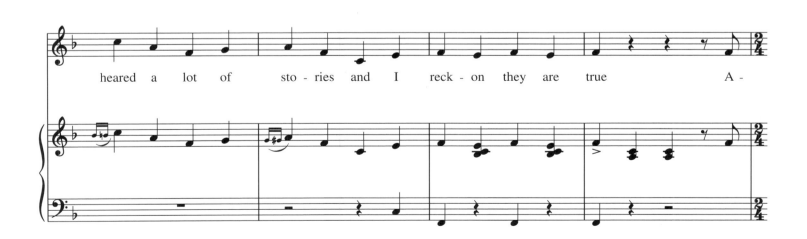

bout how girls 're put up-on by men.   I

know I mus-n't fall in-to the pit, _____ But when I'm with a fel-ler, I fer-

git!

I'm jist a girl who cain't say no,
I'm jist a girl who cain't say no,

I'm in a tur - ri - ble fix ___
Cain't seem to say it at all ___

I al - ways say, "Come on, le's go,"
I hate to dis - ser - point a beau

Jist when I or - ta say "nix!" ___ When a
When he is pay - in' a call. ___ Fer a

per - son tries to kiss a girl, I
while I ack re - fined and cool, A -

know she or-ta give his face a smack. _____ But as
set-tin' on the vel-ve-teen set-tee _____ 'Nen I

soon as some-one kiss-es me, I
think of thet ol' gold-en rule, And

some-how sort-a want-a kiss him back! _____
do fer him whut he would do fer me! _____

I'm jist a fool when lights are low,
I caint re-sist a Ro-me-o,

A COCKEYED OPTIMIST
from *South Pacific*

Lyrics by Oscar Hammerstein II
Music by Richard Rodgers

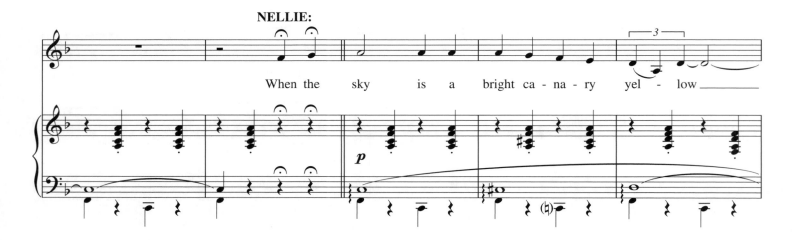

NELLIE:

When the sky is a bright ca-na-ry yel - low

I for-get ev-'ry cloud I've ev-er seen _____ So they

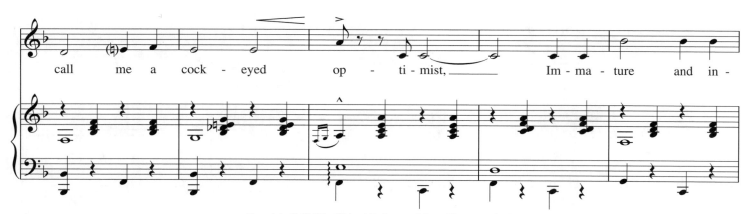

call me a cock - eyed op - ti-mist, _____ Im - ma-ture and in -

A WONDERFUL GUY

from *South Pacific*

Lyrics by Oscar Hammerstein II
Music by Richard Rodgers

And they'll say I'm na - ive As a babe to be - lieve An - y

fa - ble I hear from a per - son in pants

Fear - less - ly I'll face them and

ar - gue their doubts a - way _____

Loud - ly I'll sing a - bout flow - ers and spring _____

Flat - ly I'll

stand on my lit - tle flat feet and say _____

Love is a grand and a beau - ti - ful

thing.

I'm not a - shamed to re - veal

The world fa - mous

feel - ing I feel

REFRAIN
a tempo

I'm as corn - y as Kan - sas in Au - gust,

I'm as nor - mal as blue - ber - ry pie, No more a

smart lit - tle girl with no heart, I have found me a won - der - ful

gay As a dai - sy in May, A cli - ché com - ing true!

I'm bro - mid - ic and bright As a moon - hap - py

night Pour - ing light on the dew! _____ I'm as

corn - y as Kan - sas in Au - gust, High as a flag on the

fourth of Ju - ly! If you'll ex - cuse an ex - pres - sion I

use, I'm in love, I'm in love, I'm in love, I'm in love, I'm in

pp *molto cresc.*

love with a won - der - ful guy!

f

HONEY BUN

from *South Pacific*

Lyrics by Oscar Hammerstein II
Music by Richard Rodgers

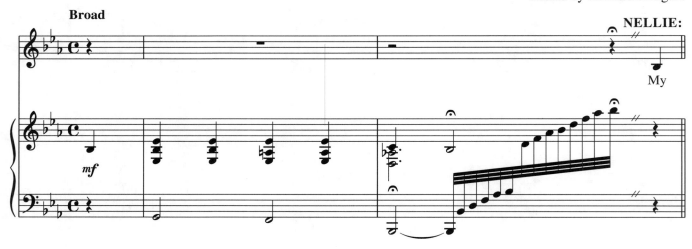

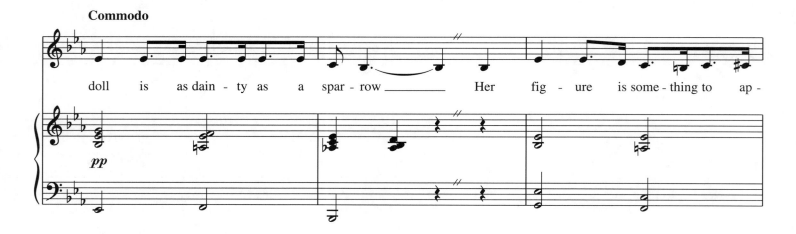

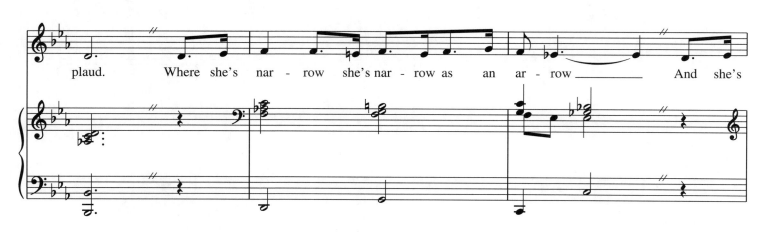

77

BALI HA'I
from *South Pacific*

Lyrics by Oscar Hammerstein II
Music by Richard Rodgers

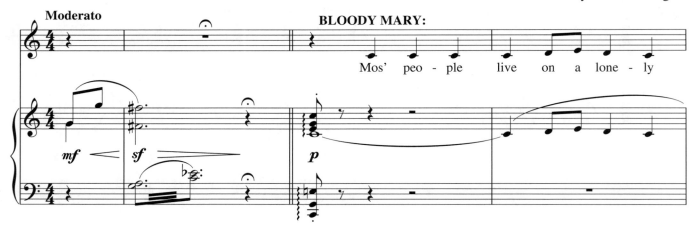

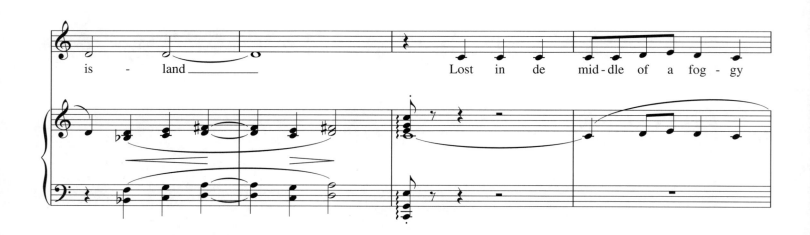

MY FAVORITE THINGS

from *The Sound of Music*

Lyrics by Oscar Hammerstein II
Music by Richard Rodgers

bee stings, When I'm feel - ing sad, _____ I

sim - ply re - mem - ber my fa - vor - ite things and then I don't

feel _____ so bad! _____

_____ Girls in white

dress - es with blue sat - in sash - es, Snow - flakes that stay on my

nose and eye - lash - es, Sil - ver white win - ters that melt in - to

springs, These are a few of my fa - vor - ite things.

When the dog bites, When the bee stings,

IT MIGHT AS WELL BE SPRING
from *State Fair*

Lyrics by Oscar Hammerstein II
Music by Richard Rodgers

MARGY: The things I used to like I don't like an-y-more, I want a lot of oth-er things I nev-er had be-fore. It's just like Mo-ther says, I sit a-round and mope, pre-

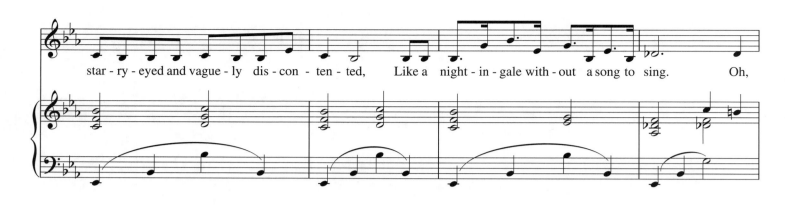

star - ry - eyed and vague - ly dis - con - ten - ted, Like a night - in - gale with - out a song to sing. Oh,

why should I have spring fe - ver when it is - n't e - ven spring?

Con moto

I keep wish - ing I were some - where else, walk - ing down a strange new street,

poco rall.

Hear - ing words that I have nev - er heard from a man I've yet to meet. I'm as

poco rall.

RODGERS & HAMMERSTEIN

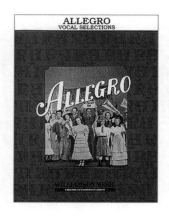

ALLEGRO
Vocal Score
00312006. . . . . . $65.00

Vocal Selections
00312007. . . . . . $10.95

FLOWER DRUM SONG
Vocal Score
00312141. . . . . . $65.00

Vocal Selections
00312140. . . . . . $14.95

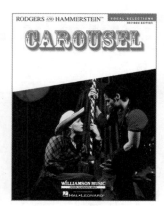

CAROUSEL
Vocal Score
01121001. . . . . . $65.00

Vocal Selections
01121008. . . . . . $14.95

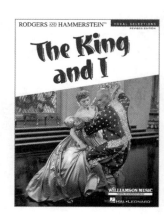

THE KING AND I
Vocal Score
00312228. . . . . . $65.00

Vocal Selections
00312227. . . . . . $14.95

Souvenir Folio Edition
00313067. . . . . . $15.95

CINDERELLA
Vocal Score
00312092. . . . . . $65.00

Vocal Selections
00312091. . . . . . $14.95

Vocal Selections (Disney)
00313095. . . . . . $10.95

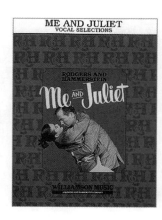

ME AND JULIET
Vocal Score
00312255. . . . . . $65.00

Vocal Selections
00312256. . . . . . $10.95

RODGERS & HAMMERSTEIN

OKLAHOMA!

Vocal Score
00312294. . . .$65.00

Vocal Selections
00312292. . . .$14.95

Commemorative
Edition
01121041. . . .$16.95

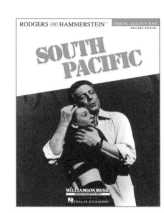

SOUTH PACIFIC

Vocal Score
00312401. . . .$65.00

Vocal Selections
00312400. . . .$14.99

Souvenir Folio Edition
00313418. . . .$14.95

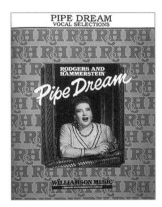

PIPE DREAM

Vocal Score
00312321. . . .$65.00

Vocal Selections
00312320. . . .$10.95

STATE FAIR

Vocal Selections
00312403. . . .$14.95

THE SOUND OF MUSIC

Vocal Score
00312391. . . .$65.00

Vocal Selections
00312392. . . .$16.99

Souvenir Folio Edition
00313114. . . .$16.99

ABOUT THE ENHANCED CDs

In addition to performances and piano accompaniments playable on both your CD player and computer, these enhanced CDs also include tempo adjustment software for computer use only. This software, known as Amazing Slow Downer, was originally created for use in pop music to allow singers and players the freedom to independently adjust both tempo and pitch elements. Because we believe there may be valuable educational use for these features in classical and theatre music, we have included this software as a tool for both the teacher and student. For quick and easy installation instructions of this software, please see below.

In recording a piano accompaniment we necessarily must choose one tempo. Our choice of tempo, phrasing, ritardandos, and dynamics is carefully considered. But by the nature of recording, it is only one option.

However, we encourage you to explore your own interpretive ideas, which may differ from our recordings. This new software feature allows you to adjust the tempo up and down without affecting the pitch. We recommend that this tempo adjustment feature be used with care and insight.

The audio quality may be somewhat compromised when played through the Amazing Slow Downer. This compromise in quality will not be a factor in playing the CD audio track on a normal CD player or through another audio computer program.

INSTALLATION INSTRUCTIONS:

For Macintosh OS 8, 9 and X:
• Load the CD-ROM into your CD-ROM Drive on your computer.
• Each computer is set up a little differently. Your computer may automatically open the audio CD portion of this enhanced CD and begin to play it.
• To access the CD-ROM features, double-click on the data portion of the CD-ROM (which will have the Hal Leonard icon in red and be named as the book).
• Double-click on the "Amazing OS 8 (9 or X)" folder.
• Double-click "Amazing Slow Downer"/"Amazing X PA" to run the software from the CD-ROM, or copy this file to your hard disk and run it from there.
• Follow the instructions on-screen to get started. The Amazing Slow Downer should display tempo, pitch and mix bars. Click to select your track and adjust pitch or tempo by sliding the appropriate bar to the left or to the right.

For Windows:
• Load the CD-ROM into your CD-ROM Drive on your computer.
• Each computer is set up a little differently. Your computer may automatically open the audio CD portion of this enhanced CD and begin to play it.
• To access the CD-ROM features, click on My Computer then right click on the Drive that you placed the CD in. Click Open. You should then see a folder named "Amazing Slow Downer". Click to open the "Amazing Slow Downer" folder.
• Double-click "setup.exe" to install the software from the CD-ROM to your hard disk. Follow the on-screen instructions to complete installation.
• Go to "Start," "Programs" and find the "Amazing Slow Downer" folder. Go to that folder and select the "Amazing Slow Downer" software.
• Follow the instructions on-screen to get started. The Amazing Slow Downer should display tempo, pitch and mix bars. Click to select your track and adjust pitch or tempo by sliding the appropriate bar to the left or to the right.
• Note: On Windows NT, 2000, XP, and Vista, the user should be logged in as the "Administrator" to guarantee access to the CD-ROM drive. Please see the help file for further information.

MINIMUM SYSTEM REQUIREMNTS:

For Macintosh:
Power Macintosh; Mac OS 8.5 or higher; 4 MB Application RAM; 8x Multi-Session CD-ROM drive

For Windows:
Pentium, Celeron or equivalent processor; Windows 95, 98, ME, NT, 2000, XP, Vista; 4 MB Application RAM; 8x Multi-Session CD-ROM drive